Love for Logan

By Award-Winning Author Lori DeMonia
Illustrated by Monique Turchan

Halo
PUBLISHING
INTERNATIONAL

ISBN: 978-1-61244-359-1
Library of Congress Control Number: 2015905331

Printed in the United States of America

Halo Publishing International
1100 NW Loop 410
Suite 700 - 176
San Antonio, Texas 78213
1-877-705-9647
www.halopublishing.com
contact@halopublishing.com

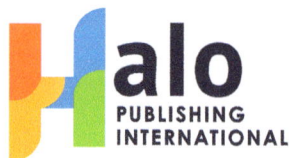

For Leah – the *true* inspiration behind this story.

I'm too excited to sit still! I finally get to put my pink butterfly costume and sparkle wings on tonight for my ballet recital. I can't wait for everyone to see me. But, I'm worried too. What if my whole family won't be there? It won't be as fun if they *all* can't watch me dance. My tummy is flip-flopping! You see, my sister Leah has autism. Some places and noises upset her. Like, if a motorcycle rides by, she will cover her ears and yell, "Sorry!" I think it's kinda cute she yells *sorry*. I wish they *could* say they're *sorry* for hurting her ears! I hope she'll be able to go to the theater. I'm trying hard not to wiggle while Mom puts my hair into a bun. I asked my sister to read me a story while I'm stuck here.

"You found your doll? How wonderful! And she looks just like you! The End," Leah read to me.

"Thanks Leah," I said. "I liked that story."

She looked up and smiled. "I like your hair."

"Thank you Leah. Is it done, Mom?" I asked.

"We're all done," Mom answered.

I jumped up and ran to the mirror. Just then, Daddy walked in.

"Hi Daddy. I'm glad you're home," I said, seeing him in the mirror.

"Wow, look at you!" he said.

"Mom just finished my hair. Don't I look like a real ballerina?" I asked.

"You sure do," he answered.

When I spun around from the mirror, I spilled the metal tin full of bobby pins. Leah jumped up, covered her ears, and ran to her room.

"I'm sorry Leah," I yelled. "I didn't mean to scare you."

"It's OK Logan, it was an accident," Mom said.

I helped Mom pick up the bobby pins.

"Could we talk to you about something?" Mom asked.

"Sure, about what?"

"You see how some noises upset your sister?" Dad asked.

"Yeah, I didn't mean to," I said.

"We know, and we'd like to explain that along with autism, your sister has what's called *sensory processing disorder*."

"What's that?" I asked.

"It's a condition that makes someone react differently than what we'd expect. If they're sensitive to things they taste, touch, or hear, like what you just saw, they respond in a way that's different from you or me," Mom explained.

"Do *all* kids with autism have it?" I asked.

"Many do, but it's a disorder anyone could have," Daddy answered. "Leah's sensitive to loud sounds, but you know what?"

"What?" I asked.

"Her class field trip was to a *bowling alley* once–" he began.

"But bowling alleys are super noisy!" I said.

"I know - but, she went and had a great time!" Dad explained.

"Wow, that's cool!" I said. "Why was that different?"

"Maybe when she wants to be included, it helps her overcome this sometimes," Mom answered.

"Telling her what to expect helps too," Daddy added. "Sudden loud noises, like fire drills at school, upset her because they're unexpected."

"So, just sounds upset her?" I asked.

"Not just sounds," Daddy said. "Do you remember when we tried taking a picture of both of you wearing the sweaters Grandma knit you?" Daddy asked.

"Yeah, Leah wouldn't put that ugly thing on," I said.

"It wasn't what they *looked* like, but because they're wool, and scratchy. She's sensitive that way too," Daddy explained. "What she touches, or feels on her skin."

"Is *that* why you take labels out of her clothes, Mom?" I asked.

"Exactly," Mom said.

"So, as much as we all want to be there tonight, I'm sorry honey, we just can't promise," Daddy said. "I hope you understand."

"I do," I answered.

Daddy put his arm around my shoulder. "I'll talk with her, tell her what to expect, and see how she feels about going."

"All right Daddy."

11

My lip quivered as I tried hard not to cry. I didn't want Leah to be scared, but if my *whole* family won't be watching, it's going to be hard to float like a happy butterfly tonight. Maybe no one will notice.

Before leaving, I went past Leah's room. Mom was putting out one of Leah's dresses. She winked at me, "Just in case."

I smiled. Mom always believes in my sister. She says, *before thinking your sister can't, give her a try first.* That's what I'll do. Give Leah a *try* first!

I'm finally at the theater. Backstage was noisy with all the talking and giggling. And it smelled like the candy aisle at the grocery store from all the fruity lip gloss and hairspray. Girls were stretching their legs and flexing their toes. I spotted the girls in my group. I zig zagged through the crowd, trying not to poke anybody with my wings. Together, we looked like a flock of pink butterflies.

"Good luck sweetheart. You'll do great!" Mom said, giving me a thumbs up.

"Thanks Mom!" I yelled as she walked to the door.

Our teacher took us to our places on stage. I'm on the very end. I slowly moved the curtain, taking a peek. I spotted Mom in the front row, but she was looking the other way. Then, she popped out of her seat. She started waving. I looked far in the back.

Oh my gosh! Leah's walking down the aisle! Wearing her dress! She's carrying flowers, *and* smiling! Daddy's following her. "They made it! They made it!" I whispered, feeling a rush in my belly.

The lights dimmed. I pulled my hand away, letting the curtain close and sprang back to my spot. The curtain slowly opened.

"Aww!" said the audience.

Finally, the curtain opened all the way. There's my *whole* family! As our music began to play, I saw Leah st*ill* smiling! We twirled, jumped, and leaped across the stage. I felt like I was floating in the air. After our dance we held hands and curtsied. This was just what I wished for--my family, all here to watch me. I waved to them as the curtain closed.

I waited backstage for them. Leah spotted me first and dashed over.

"Here you go Logan!" she said, flinging the big bouquet of tulips at me.

"Thank you so much Leah! I'm happy you're here!" I said, giving her a hug.

Mom hugged me too. "You did wonderful sweetie."

Daddy kissed my forehead. "You danced beautifully tonight, Logan."

Back at home, we had my favorite, pepperoni pizza with extra cheese! While eating our pizza, Leah and I were humming songs and swinging our legs under the table. It felt like we both had something to celebrate.

At bedtime, I told Daddy goodnight. "Thanks for being there tonight. I'm glad Leah was there too."

"You're welcome, Logan. I'm so proud of you! You're a graceful ballerina *and* a wonderful sister."

"Thanks Daddy. Goodnight," I said as I gave him a hug.

Mom followed to tuck me in bed.

First, I stopped by my sister's room to say goodnight, but she was already asleep. I tiptoed over to her bed as Mom waited in the doorway.

"Goodnight Leah. You're the best sister ever," I whispered, softly kissing her cheek.

Before I tiptoed out of her room, I glanced at her art easel and saw a painting of a ballerina.

"Look Mom," I whispered, pointing to it.

"Wow, how beautiful!" she said. "You must have inspired her."

"Do you think if I teach Leah some ballet steps she'd show me how to paint?" I asked.

"I bet she'd like that," Mom answered.

I climbed into bed. Before Mom turned off the lights I asked, "Why wasn't Leah upset tonight?"

"I don't know for sure, but I think it was her *love.*"

"*Her love*?" I asked.

"Your sister loves you *so much* and wanted to be a part of your special night. Showing her support for *you* was what mattered. Daddy said she even *asked* to bring you flowers!"

"That's awesome!" I said." I'm *so* glad Leah's *my* big sister!"

Mom hugged me. "And *I know* Leah's glad you're her, *little* sister, too, Logan!"

www.ingramcontent.com/pod-product-compliance
Lightning Source LLC
LaVergne TN
LVHW070836080426
835509LV00027B/3488